This is God's starting point with us:
right where we are.

And that's where we're starting too:
with the outrageously beautiful truth
that our whole lives matter to the
Lord of all things.

Our whole lives.

Nothing left out.

licc. | [fusion]

ROUTED

JOURNEYING INTO WORK WITH GOD

PARTICIPANT'S WORKBOOK

ROUTED

Routed is a student discipleship resource for finalists. It shows you that the whole of your life matters to God and equips you for the transition out of university and into work.

Scripture quotations taken from the Holy Bible, New International Version Anglicised Copyright © 1979, 1984, 2011 Biblica. Used by permission of Hodder & Stoughton Ltd, an Hachette UK company. All rights reserved. 'NIV' is a registered trademark of Biblica UK trademark number 1448790.

licc. | [fusion]

'IF IT BE NOT NOW, YET IT WILL COME. THE READINESS IS ALL.'

Hamlet, William Shakespeare

How would you prepare for a trip to Everest's base camp?

Buy some new hiking boots? Go into altitude training? Find a trustworthy guide?

Whether you're a future Bear Grylls or can't stand the thought of a night in the wild, life (especially life with Jesus) holds adventures for everyone. And if you're reading this, you're probably about to embark on one of them: moving on from uni into the world of work.

Routed: Journeying into Work with God is all about helping you to prepare for this next life adventure. Think of it like a handy backpack (or suitcase if that's more your style), full of equipment and provisions for the road ahead.

Routed will help you to understand God's interest in the whole of your life, to integrate your faith with everyday work, to choose work wisely, and to navigate change healthily.

When it comes to the adventure of starting work, 'the readiness is all'. Even small adjustments made as you prepare for this period of transition act like the needle of a compass, setting a good course for the road ahead: decades of partnership with God in his great mission to renew and restore all things.

Welcome to *Routed*. May joy, grace, and wisdom be yours on the journey!

Dom Palmer, Nell Goddard, & Charles Hippsley

LICC

P.S. You can access the leader's guide and videos at **licc.org.uk/routed***.*

CONTENTS

ROUTED INTO FRUITFULNESS

Section	Title	Mins
REFLECTION	GOD IN THE DAY-TO-DAY	10
ACTIVITY	LOOKING AT THE ROAD AHEAD	20
CORE CONTENT	ON THE HORIZON: FRONTLINES	20
DISCUSSION	THE 6MS OF FRUITFULNESS	15
INTERVIEW	CHRIS' STORY: WORST DAY AT THE OFFICE	15
PRAYER	LIFE NOW AND THE ROAD AHEAD	10
JOURNEYING ON	FRONTLINES: CONNECT THE DOTS	DO LATER

God in the day-to-day

10 mins

Read the psalm together

The Lord is my shepherd,
I lack nothing.

He makes me lie down in green pastures,
he leads me beside quiet waters,
he refreshes my soul.

He guides me along the right paths
for his name's sake.
Even though I walk through the darkest valley,
I will fear no evil, for you are with me;
your rod and your staff,
they comfort me.

You prepare a table before me
in the presence of my enemies.
You anoint my head with oil;
my cup overflows.

Surely your goodness and love will follow me
all the days of my life,
and I will dwell in the house of the Lord forever.

Discuss

- This psalm describes various parts of David's life where God has met with him. Which ones can you see here?

- If God met with David in all these parts of his life, what might that mean for where we can meet with God in our daily lives?

'HOW CAN ANYONE
REMAIN INTERESTED
IN A RELIGION WHICH
SEEMS TO HAVE
NO CONCERN WITH NINE-
TENTHS OF THEIR LIFE?'

DOROTHY L. SAYERS
WHY WORK (1942)

Looking at the road ahead

20 mins

What do you expect to happen in your life between now and the end of your first year after graduation?

Use the space below to write a list, make a timeline, or draw a roadmap – whatever helps you think and imagine well. Record the events, studies, celebrations, work, etc. that you expect to happen.

Discuss in groups of 2 or 3

- Which areas of your roadmap feel exciting?
  Why? (mark them with an E)

- Which areas feel worrying?
  Why? (mark them with a W)

- Do any areas feel exciting and worrying at the same time?
  Why?

Read this prayer together

Lord Jesus, you are our Good Shepherd.

You lead us down the right paths,
even when we only see a maze.
You are the Lord of all that is past, all that is now,
and all that is to come,
The Lord of all our hopes, and all our fears.

Loving Father, every detail of our life is significant to you:
Our rest, our study, our relationships,
Our hobbies, our struggles, our dreams.
We commit to your care everything we've written here:
Everything we expect to happen as you lead us on in life,
And everything we cannot yet imagine.

Holy Spirit, lead us in our time together:
Direct our wayward hearts to focus on their Shepherd, Jesus Christ.
Open our eyes to see your creativity in the now,
And lead us into a greater vision of what's to come,
That we would be fruitful in you wherever we go,
And see your kingdom come wherever we are.

To the glory of your name may it be, O Lord.
Amen.

On the horizon: frontlines

20 mins

Our frontlines are the places we normally go through the week, meeting the people we normally meet (particularly those who don't know Jesus), and doing the things we normally do.

 **WATCH**
On the horizon: frontlines

 **READ**
Colossians 1:15-20

KEY POINTS

Colossians 1 tells us that all of life matters to God, not just the 'holy' bits

God loves to work in and through us wherever we are on a day-to-day basis: what we call our frontlines

Jesus is Lord over everywhere we go and everything we do – and this doesn't change when your frontlines change

Discuss

- Where are your frontlines now, at uni?

- Where in your life now do you find it harder to see God at work? Why do you think that is?

- Looking at your roadmap, what new frontlines might you have in the next couple of years? (e.g. workplace, bus stop, house, gym)

The 6Ms of fruitfulness

15 mins

One of the great joys of being a Christian is realising that God chooses to work in and through us, wherever we are.

One of the harder things, however, is being able to spot it. Many of us just don't have the eyes to see how we are already being fruitful for Christ in our daily lives. So here's a framework to help you see how God is already working through you, and to inspire your imagination for how he might in the future. It's not a 'to-do list' but an encouragement; a lens through which to look at life with fresh eyes.

Ask yourself: how am I...?

M1 *Modelling godly character*

The fruit of the Spirit (Galatians 5:22-23) at work in your actions, words, and thoughts

M2 *Making good work*

Doing everything to and for the glory of God

M3 *Ministering grace and love*

Going the extra mile for others

M4 *Moulding culture*

Finding ways to make changes for the better

M5 *Being a Mouthpiece for truth and justice*

Combatting lies, snuffing out gossip, working for justice

M6 *Being a Messenger of the gospel*

Sharing the hope that you have in Jesus and the difference he makes to your life

INTERVIEW

Chris' story: worst day at the office

15 mins

WATCH
Chris' Story

Reflect on which of the 6Ms listed on the previous page you can see exhibited in Chris' story of working life.

Discuss in groups of 2 or 3

- Which of the 6Ms can you see in your life already?

- In what ways do the 6Ms help you to see other opportunities to be fruitful on your uni frontlines?

- Choose 2-3 things you marked with W on your roadmap. Can you see opportunities there for you to be fruitful in one or more of the 6Ms?

  Example: When looking for a job there are opportunities to 'model godly character' during applications and interviews.

PRAYER

Life now and the road ahead

10 mins

Pray in small groups using the following pointers

- **Life Now:** Choose one of your current frontlines, and one of the 6Ms you'd like to exhibit more in that context next week.

- **The Road Ahead:** Using your roadmaps, choose something you marked with an E and something you marked with a W.

JOURNEYING ON

Frontlines: connect the dots

Optional personal study for in between sessions

 READ
Colossians 1:15-20 again

- Read it a second time, bringing to mind or writing down the frontlines (and their people and situations) that make up your life's 'all things'.

- Pray for God's kingdom to come on those frontlines.

- Put your 6M card somewhere that you'll see it regularly, a desk, noticeboard, fridge door... Whenever you spot it, thank God that he is working in and through you in your daily life and ask for his help in the week ahead.

'Not only that, but all the broken and dislocated pieces of the universe — people and things, animals and atoms — get properly fixed and fit together in vibrant harmonies, all because of his death, his blood that poured down from the cross.'

COLOSSIANS 1:20, THE MESSAGE

---- SESSION 2 ----

ROUTED INTO WORK

Section	Title	Mins
REFLECTION	COMFORT AND CHALLENGE	10
ACTIVITY	THE TIME OF YOUR (WORKING) LIFE	5
CORE CONTENT	ON THE HORIZON: WORK	25
INTERVIEW	DOM'S STORY: A WORK IN PROGRESS	5
DISCUSSION	WHATEVER YOU DO	20
PRAYER	LIFE NOW AND THE ROAD AHEAD	15
JOURNEYING ON	COLOSSIANS 3: GOING DEEPER	DO LATER

Comfort and challenge

10 mins

Read the psalm together

The Lord is my shepherd,
I lack nothing.

He makes me lie down in green pastures,
he leads me beside quiet waters,
he refreshes my soul.

He guides me along the right paths
for his name's sake.
Even though I walk through the darkest valley,
I will fear no evil, for you are with me;
your rod and your staff,
they comfort me.

You prepare a table before me
in the presence of my enemies.
You anoint my head with oil;
my cup overflows.

Surely your goodness and love will follow me
all the days of my life,
and I will dwell in the house of the Lord forever.

Fill it out

Looking at Psalm 23, make a list of situations mentioned in the psalm that are comforting and situations are challenging.

Comforting	Challenging

Now, go back through your table and the psalm, and put a tick next to the places and situations in which David says God is present.

In this session, we're going to explore God's invitation to work alongside him in our daily lives. It's an exciting vision, but we're also going to consider how it works itself out in both comforting and challenging workplace situations, as we live and work in a broken world.

The time of your (working) life

5 mins

Take a few minutes to work out how much time you expect to spend on some important areas in post-uni life. This isn't about making a hard-and-fast life schedule; it's just a starting point to help you think ahead. The total number of hours in a week is 7x24 = 168.

Activity	How many hours per day?	How many days per week?	Total hours per week
Cooking/eating			
Sleeping			
Working (Assume 9-5, Mon-Fri, if you're not sure)			
Commuting (Assume 1 hour each way if you're not sure)			
Church service			
Mid-week church group			
Total waking hours per week:			
Total work-related hours per week:			
Total church-related hours per week:			

Does anything stand out to you or surprise you about these numbers?

CORE CONTENT

On the horizon: work

25 mins

Discuss

● What does the thought of **work** bring to your mind?

WATCH
On the Horizon: Work

KEY POINTS

In Genesis 1, we see God the worker creating a context in which all things can flourish. And then he delegates the care and cultivation of his creation to humankind

This means that our work is a key part of God's creative and restorative purposes, through his people, in his world

Christians often find it difficult to believe that their daily work is significant to God

But work is full of opportunities to live with and for God:

● The work itself getting things done in the world that God wants done

● Becoming more like Jesus within the workplace environment

● As a context for mission and ministry (remember the 6Ms!)

Discuss

Work was designed to be:

Creative:
Bringing order, making provision, creating beauty, releasing potential, bringing joy (creating a context for life to flourish)

Restorative:
Helping to put right things that are broken as a result of human sin, for example health, relationships, structures in society, etc.

If you have a job lined up, or an idea of your future work, hold that in mind. If you don't yet have a clear next step, think about either an application of your degree, or a previous experience of work (e.g. part-time/holiday jobs).

● How might your future work take part in God's creative activity?

● How might your future work align with God's restorative purposes?

Examples

Teacher

Creative: releasing the potential of future generations, helping them flourish in life, and bringing order and understanding to complex subjects

Restorative: being an encouraging and good adult figure for children, working with parents, local services, and others to foster positive school and larger community culture

Barista

Creative: creating beauty and enjoyment, providing sustenance for people through a well made coffee

Restorative: making customers feel valued and appreciated (for some of whom it may be the only human contact during that day)

Software developer

Creative: bringing order to information and processes, creating tools that release the potential of organisations and people in many areas of human endeavour, bringing ease of use, and joy (in the case of games or design)

Restorative: reducing waste and human error, fixing broken or inadequate systems, creating tools that extend access to education, information, and communications, creating solutions for disabilities, protecting against crime and misinformation

Dom's story: a work in progress

5 mins

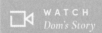 **WATCH**
Dom's Story

KEY POINTS

There are two prevailing myths in our culture:

- The Myth of Instant Everything encourages us to believe that we can and should have anything we want immediately

- The Myth of Comparison encourages us to believe that we can and should measure ourselves by comparing ourselves to others

Both of these myths are just that – myths! A lot of the really important things in life don't come quickly – think friendship, skills, or jobs. Comparison is the thief of joy, and pushes us into self-centredness and selfishness

Embrace the fact that you are a work in progress, in the hands of a good God

Use Dom's Story to help you engage with the extract you'll read next from Colossians 3, especially through the video's lens of 'work myths' (powerful cultural stories): instant everything and comparison.

DISCUSSION

Whatever you do

20 mins

READ
Colossians 3:23-24

Discuss

- What wisdom does this passage provide to someone who isn't feeling 'successful', or doing the job they wanted to do straight away?

- What wisdom does this passage provide to someone who feels trapped in comparing their life to others' lives?

- What might working 'with all your heart, as working for the Lord' look like for you in a new stage of life? (Think about previous job experiences or examples if that helps.)

When we scratch the surface of the two 'work myths', we uncover the human desires for significance and relationship, twisted out of shape and misdirected.

Colossians 3 instructs us to 'work for the Lord' rather than for 'success' or a massive Instagram story. It also promises a future inheritance from God and the present reality of working in relationship with Jesus. By doing this, it speaks to the desires beneath the 'work myths' – desires for significance and relationship – and moves us towards a vision of work as wholehearted service.

Life now and the road ahead

15 mins

Pray in groups of 2 or 3

- **Life Now:** How do you respond to the thought of embracing your life as a 'work in progress'? Pray for each other about starting that now.

- **The Road Ahead:** Look/think back to your reflections in 'Why does my work matter to God?'. Pray blessing over each other's future work.

Read this prayer together

Father, Creator of all things,
We recognise that we are your creatures
Unable to live without you, called to work with you.
We bring before you our expectations about work,
Trusting that you lovingly hold our whole lives together,
And trusting that we were made to bear fruit for your glory.

Jesus, living Word of God,
We praise you for your great creativity and restoration.
May our daily work go with the grain of your Kingdom,
Creating space for life to flourish,
And bringing glory to your name.

Holy Spirit, sustainer and friend,
We thank you for your loving presence,
Both in times of confidence, and in times of confusion.
Give us eyes to see the opportunities in this new stage,
To encounter you, to learn from you, and to minister to others.

Establish the work of our hands, great God,
To your glory, Amen

JOURNEYING ON

Colossians 3: going deeper

Optional personal study for in between sessions

- Think about a previous experience of work – studying
  for your degree, summer work, or another job.

 READ
Colossians 3:17, 23-24 slowly

- Underline any words or phrases in the passages that
  you found difficult to put into practice then.
  *Example: you might underline, 'not only when their eye is
  on you' if self-motivation was/is a challenge for you.*

- How could you do those things differently in
  this next season of work? Talk to God about
  that and write some thoughts down.

ROUTED THROUGH CALLING

Section	Title	Mins
REFLECTION	FINDING OUR WAY	10
CORE CONTENT	ON THE HORIZON: CALLING	25
INTERVIEW	SARAH-JANE'S STORY: ONE CALLING	20
ACTIVITY	WHAT'S IN MY HANDS?	25
PRAYER	LIFE NOW AND THE ROAD AHEAD	10
JOURNEYING ON	WHAT'S IN MY HANDS?	DO LATER

Finding our way

10 mins

Read the psalm together

The Lord is my shepherd,
I lack nothing.

He makes me lie down in green pastures,
he leads me beside quiet waters,
he refreshes my soul.

He guides me along the right paths
for his name's sake.
Even though I walk through the darkest valley,
I will fear no evil, for you are with me;
your rod and your staff, they comfort me.

You prepare a table before me
in the presence of my enemies.
You anoint my head with oil;
my cup overflows.

Surely your goodness and love will follow me
all the days of my life,
and I will dwell in the house of the Lord forever.

Discuss

- Look closely at the second stanza. What three things does David declare that God gives him, whatever the situation?

- How does this help us if our way ahead after university is not as clear cut or obvious as we'd hoped?

CORE CONTENT

On the horizon: calling

25 mins

Discuss

- What does the word **calling** bring to mind?

WATCH
On the Horizon: Calling

KEY POINTS

- We're called, first and foremost, to some*one* rather than some*thing* – God calls people to himself

- Our primary calling to Christ then overflows into all of life, shaping how we make decisions about what work we do, and how we do the work itself

- If the heart of our call is to follow Jesus, we don't need to be anxious about getting stuck in 'God's plan B' for us, as we entrust our work and our lives to him

- Rather than asking 'what can I gain from my career – how much money or status can I achieve for myself?' we can now ask 'what have I already been given, that I can offer, so that other people can flourish?'

Discuss

- Think back to your discussion on calling at the beginning of this session. Have your thoughts changed? If so, how?

- How might we be freed up to seek God's guidance and to help others flourish by understanding that our primary calling is to follow Jesus?

- The video suggests 'What have I got in my hands?' as a way of approaching work and job-hunting. Do you find that a helpful question? Why or why not?

INTERVIEW

Sarah-Jane's story: one calling

20 mins

WATCH
Sarah-Jane's Story

Discuss

- What stood out to you, surprised you, or encouraged you from Sarah-Jane's story?

- Sarah-Jane mentions three main ways that her primary calling to Christ affects her day-to-day working life:
  1. Unchanging assurance of value
  2. Significance in everyday tasks
  3. Sharing faith through sharing life

- Do any of these feel particularly relevant or significant to you? Why?

What's in my hands?

25 mins

This diagram is a way of helping you begin to understand what makes you unique, and how you can offer yourself in service to God and others through your work. We'll start fleshing it out in this session, but to get the best out of it, we recommend you continue filling it in on your own.

Discuss in groups of 2 or 3

● When considering your suitability for a job, which of the above questions are you drawn to, and which ones feel less obvious or easy to think about? Why might that be?

Fill it out

Now, spend the next 10 minutes beginning to fill
out the 'What's in my hands?' diagram on the next
page – but don't expect to finish in that time!

To help you start, especially with 'What am I good at?' and 'What
experiences do I have?', think about one current or previous
experience you enjoyed and ask yourself the following questions:

● What activities/tasks did you enjoy the most?

● What did you learn about what you were good at?

Discuss in pairs

After 10 minutes, find a partner and begin to talk it over. Again,
don't expect to cover all the questions during this session.

What do I care deeply about?

What am I good at?

What are my character traits, good and bad?

WHAT'S IN MY HANDS?

What experiences do I have?

What kind of personality do I have?

What contacts have I got?

Life now and the road ahead

10 mins

Pray in groups of 2 or 3

- **Life Now:** Think of a situation coming up where you could use one of the things you wrote down to the glory of God and to serve others. Pray for that situation.

- **The Road Ahead:** What has God shown you in this session about how he's made you and how you can serve him and others through your work? Pray blessing over those things.

Read this prayer together

Almighty God, the earth is yours, and everything in it.
You have made each of us to bear your image,
Each with uniquely precious gifts and stories,
Fearful and wonderful, known and loved.
And you have called each of us to yourself,
Adopting us as your children, and apprenticing us to your Son.
Wonderful indeed are your works, O God!

Incomparable Jesus, the maker and sustainer of all things,
We marvel at your great imagination,
And we wonder at your comprehensive redemption.
You are utterly committed to our flourishing;
If we ever doubt it, show us again your cross.
May we likewise be utterly committed
to the flourishing of others.

Renewing Spirit, who in the beginning hovered over the deep,
Brood over our lives with your loving presence.
Renew our hearts and minds,
and help us to offer ourselves to you completely:
Our skills, our stories, our passions, our dreams,
Everything that you have placed in our hands.

To your glory may it be, O God. Amen.

JOURNEYING ON

What's in my hands?

Optional personal study for in between sessions

Continue filling in the diagram you began on page 39. Take time and quiet over it, ask for God's help, and engage with the wisdom of people who know you well. This diagram, and the insights you gain from it, can then be applied in things like:

- Job searching and applications (CVs, answering common interview questions, understanding work environments).

- Improving friendships and relationships (in and out of the workplace) through deepening understanding and self-awareness.

- Taking the bigger picture goals of your life to God.

The circles in the diagram aren't exhaustive, by the way! Other helpful questions for considering work could include:

- 'What kind of work environment do I prefer?'

- 'Where in the world/the country could I work?'

- 'What do I enjoy?'

ROUTED THROUGH CHANGE

Section	Title	Mins
REFLECTION	THE CONSTANT	10
CORE CONTENT	ON THE HORIZON: CHANGE	30
ACTIVITY	THE CHANGE GRID	20
PRAYER	LIFE NOW AND THE ROAD AHEAD	10
INTERVIEW	CHARLES' STORY: DEALING WITH CHANGE	10
PRAYER	COMMISSIONING	5

LOOKING FORWARD	RE:WORK CONFERENCE

The constant

10 mins

Read the psalm together

The Lord is my shepherd,
I lack nothing.

He makes me lie down in green pastures,
he leads me beside quiet waters,
he refreshes my soul.

He guides me along the right paths
for his name's sake.
Even though I walk through the darkest valley,
I will fear no evil, for you are with me;
your rod and your staff,
they comfort me.

You prepare a table before me
in the presence of my enemies.
You anoint my head with oil;
my cup overflows.

Surely your goodness and love will follow me
all the days of my life,
and I will dwell in the house of the Lord forever.

Discuss

- What aspects of God's presence does David name as constant throughout his life?

- How does that make you feel as you consider your own transition out of university?

'Surely your
goodness and love
will follow me all
the days of my life'

PSALM 23:6

On the horizon: change

30 mins

Discuss

What does the word **change** bring to mind?

 **WATCH**
On the Horizon: Change

 **READ**
Matthew 3:13-4:17

KEY POINTS

- God is unchanging, but understands change

- He experienced change in the person of Jesus, God on earth in human form... who even went through a career change!

- So we can take our excitement or anxieties about change to God, knowing that he fully understands and can speak into them from his eternal viewpoint

Discuss in pairs

● How does Jesus stay rooted in his identity and focused on his purpose during this time of temptations, challenges, and opportunities?

● What challenges, temptations, and opportunities do you think you will encounter as you move on from uni?

● What will help you to stay rooted and focused in identity and purpose during this time of change?

ACTIVITY

The change grid

20 mins

Read the change grid and change table on the following pages.
Fill in the change grid, using the change table for reference.

Discuss together

● What are you thankful for about uni life now?

● What are you looking forward to leaving behind?

● What opportunities can you see as you look ahead?

● What challenges can you see as you look ahead?

What am I thankful for about uni life now?

What opportunities can I see as I look ahead?

What am I looking forward to leaving behind?

What challenges can I see as I look ahead?

——————————— UNI LIFE ———————————

Time is very flexible

- You can arrange social gatherings at various times
- Boundaries between study and fun are blurred
- Year runs Sept-Sept with the same holidays for everyone

Friendships form quickly, through proximity & common interests

- Often quite intense, may involve living/studying together
- Larger circle of friends, opportunities to invest in more people

Family relationships change

- Cross between child/adult relationship with parents
- Dependence to semi-independence – away during term
- Probably still living with parents during holidays

Money can be tight

- Student loans/grants and financial support from family
- Food, rent, and bills are the only fixed outgoings
- If you're employed, it's probably only part-time

Assessment comes at clear intervals

- Clearly ranked and easily compared to others
- Mostly self-accountable for your work
- Money coming in is unaffected by your performance

Church will probably be student-specific

- Student groups have dedicated staff
- Can feel like a bit of a bubble
- Committed to two churches – at uni and at home

Evangelism is about speaking of Jesus in and through your whole life – wherever you are and whatever you're doing – but it may have felt as if it's been focused around inviting people to apologetics talks or events weeks

--------- **POST-UNI LIFE** ---------

Time is scheduled, with clear boundaries

- c.40% of your waking hours will be spent commuting or at work
- Weekends become more flexible. Embrace the joy of Saturday mornings!
- Set amount of holiday days taken at any point during the year

Friendships are based on deliberate choice, rather than proximity

- Less time for meeting up
- Can really invest in a few people, and depth and value can grow through commitment
- Work relationships are slower to form. Some colleagues won't be friends, but you'll still have a healthy working relationship
- More friends in different life stages and at different ages

Family relationships change again

- If you move away, there will be less family time
- If you move home, you have to learn to live together as adults

Money is earned

- More outgoings: rent may be higher, and tax must be paid
- More opportunities for generosity (to friends, church, or charity)

Assessment is ongoing

- Annual reviews or appraisals
- Continually learning and being assessed (but you'll be paid!)

Church is more 'general'

- No specific age-group ministry
- Can commit to a small group adding depth, community, and accountability
- More opportunities to serve and support the church

Evangelism is still about speaking of Jesus in and through your whole life – wherever you are and whatever you're doing – but it's less focused on talks and events, and more about living, working, listening to, and speaking with people on your day-to-day frontlines.

Life now and the road ahead

10 mins

Pray through the change grid on page 48 and 49

Start with the top half, which is about how uni life has formed us – both through things we've cherished and through things we can't wait to move on from.

- **Top Left: Thankfulness for good things**
  Spend time together speaking out prayers of thankfulness for these things. Taking the joys of uni life to God helps us to see his goodness, to recognise how he's made us and what makes us feel alive.

- **Top Right: Working through hard things**
  Spend time in shared silence – write, draw, or just be. Review your list and ask God to bring about reconciliation in anything you can't wait to leave behind. Ask God to help you bless the difficult areas and people of uni life and move on without bitterness and regret.

Watch Charles' Story for a way to pray over the bottom two quadrants - the opportunities and challenges ahead.

INTERVIEW

Charles' story: dealing with change

10 mins

WATCH
Charles' story

Look through the bottom two quadrants on the change grid and, using Charles' framework, pray through the upcoming changes in your life.

● **Express** the challenge you see by writing it down.
Talk to God in your heart about it. What does that challenge
stir up in you? Be open with God – he knows you already,
and you don't need to have it figured out to come to him.

● **Embrace:** Feel the weight of the pebble or the texture
of the paper in your hands. Embrace the fact that this
challenge is something you're facing, or will face. Tell
God that you recognise this challenge, and that you
will engage with it with his help, even if it's hard.

● **Entrust:** Give this challenge to God by putting your pebble
or paper in the centre of your group. You don't have to
cling onto this challenge and fix it on your own, but you
can embrace it, and then release it to God's competence.

● **Opportunity:** Now you're left with open hands.
What might God be giving you through this? What
opportunities could it bring? Ask him about it.

A prayer of commissioning

5 mins

Pray this prayer out loud together to commission each other for moving on from uni and into a new life stage.

Go, as a child of God,
To bear much fruit for our Father's glory.

Go, as a disciple of Jesus,
To seek and to serve the kingdom of our Lord wherever you are.

Go, as a bearer of the Holy Spirit,
Moved by the breath of God into a new season,
but always accompanied by his presence.

And may your life be to the praise and glory of the Lord.

Amen

LOOKING FORWARD

You are invited to...

LICC'S ANNUAL RE:WORK CONFERENCE

The workplace presents a whole host of challenges - issues of integrity and fair play, ambition and humility, navigating workplace relationships - some you may have talked about in *Routed*, and some you probably haven't.

Re:Work, LICC's annual day conference for 20-something professionals, offers a chance to explore these challenges and questions with others on the journey, and those ahead of you. It's a great time to 'check-in' once you've got stuck into working life and know the issues in your particular sector and role. You'll listen to talks, discuss in table groups, and have the chance to connect one-to-one with an older Christian mentor in a similar sector. Attendees find it a much-needed fresh look at their workplace culture, career goals, and 9-to-5 daily life.

So, come down to our Central London hub ready to worship, hear real-life stories, study the Bible, and connect with other young professionals as we seek to live for Jesus in the workplace. You are invited! Check licc.org.uk/rework for the details.

If you can't make it to London or make the dates, don't despair. Our Re:Work speakers and facilitators are available through our Re:Work on the Road Programme. Your church can now host a Re:Work evening or day conference for your 20s and 30s group. For a list of the talks and workshops contact students@licc.org.uk.

FOR SIX MONTHS LATER

The questions and activities here are intended to help you revisit your *Routed* experience and reflect on your first six months of post-uni life. Each of the three reflections should take 20-30 minutes. You can split them up or do them in one go, spending an evening alone with God.

Whether or not you get back to these, keep getting to know who God is, stay secure in the knowledge that he is worthy of relationship, and keep looking for traces of his grace in every part of your life.

REVIEW THE PAST

Remembering the roadmap

Look again at your roadmap on page 13.

Think about the expectations you had then of moving on from uni. Look at the things you marked as exciting, and things you marked as worrying.

With your roadmap in mind, spend some time responding to the questions on the next page, and talking with God about them.

What has been good since graduating?

What has been surprising since graduating?

What has been challenging since graduating?

How have I seen God at work in this time?

REVIEW THE PRESENT

God in your daily work

Look again at page 26 where you thought about how your future work might connect with God's creative and restorative purposes in the world.

If you're working now, ask yourself the same questions about your present job:

- How does my work take part in God's creative activity?

- How does my work align with God's restorative purposes?

- How do I meet with God in and through my daily work?

- What has God recently taught me about himself through my work?

Whether or not you're working now, Jesus promises that your life will be fruitful and glorifying to God as you follow him.

Look again at the 6Ms on page 16.

By filling in the charts on the next two pages, notice how God is growing fruit in your life already on your new frontlines; and dream for more.

Modelling
godly
character

Making
good work

Being a
Messenger of the
gospel

**HOW
A M
I ... ?**

Ministering
grace and love

Being a
Mouthpiece for
truth and justice

Moulding
culture

Model godly character

Make good work

Be a Messenger of the gospel

HOW COULD I...?

Minister grace and love

Be a Mouthpiece for truth and justice

Mould culture

THINK ABOUT THE FUTURE

Opportunities and challenges

Having thought about the past and the present, it's time to look ahead again with God. Think about the next six months to one year.

Opportunities

- What opportunities do you see ahead?

Notice how God is growing fruit in your life already on your new frontlines, and dream for more. Bless the opportunities and seek God's leading in them.

Challenges

- What challenges do you see ahead?

Express, embrace, and entrust the challenges to the Father

- **Express:** write a challenge on a pebble/post-it note

- **Embrace:** notice the object, recognise the challenge's presence

- **Entrust:** place it in front of you

- **Opportunity:** how might God work through this?

See page 53 for more explanation on expressing, embracing, and entrusting.

LIFE AFTER UNI

- ### SLEEP
  You need this to function as a human being, especially when you are adjusting. Try and get as much as you need as often as you can.

- ### SABBATH
  Set aside one day a week for Sabbath rest: time out from work and life admin, to be refreshed and to reconnect with God. Consider a 'digital Sabbath' too.

- ### CHURCH FAMILY
  Commit to a church family early on. Join a small group so you can know others and be known more deeply.

- ### SERVE
  Serve the body of Christ – get on a rota, join a team, give financially.

- ### BUDGET
  Make and stick to a budget – spend less than you earn.

- ### GIVE
  Give money away, no matter how little or much you make. (10% of your pre-tax income is a good start).

- ### READ SCRIPTURE
  Read a psalm a day, out loud. This is a simple, sustainable quiet-time habit to start with and build on.

- ### PRAY
  Try a 'commuting prayer'. Choose a few landmarks on your way into work and use them as 'triggers' for prayers.

- ### BRANCH OUT
  Have a variety of friends – Christian, non-Christian, work friends, church friends, hobby friends.

- ### BOOK IT IN
  Intentionally foster sustainable relationships. Show and tell how important they are to you, and get out your diary and book in another catch-up before you part ways.

FURTHER READING

On the theology of work

Thank God it's Monday
Mark Greene
A guide to flourishing in your workplace.

Every Good Endeavour
**Timothy Keller with
Katherine Leary Alsdorf**
A deeper dive into the theology of work.

Garden City
John Mark Comer
Work, rest, calling, and being
human in God's big story.

On self-awareness for your job

What Color is Your Parachute?
Richard Bolles
A classic text for job hunters, updated every year.

80,000 Hours
**Careers resources developed
by Effective Altruism**
80000hours.org

On whole-life discipleship

Fruitfulness on the Frontline
Mark Greene
Explore The 6Ms in more depth.

The London Institute for
Contemporary Christianity

About LICC

What difference does following Jesus make to our ordinary daily lives, to the things we normally do, in the places we normally spend time, with the people we usually meet? How can we live fruitfully and faithfully, sharing and showing the love and wisdom and ways of Christ right where we are?

Back in 1982, LICC was founded by one of the most influential Bible teachers and Christian leaders of the 20th century – John Stott. He and his co-founders wanted to change the story of the church in the UK and the rest of the world. To answer those questions, and change it to a story of God's people envisioned, empowered, encouraged. God's people sent into their daily contexts, confident in him, in the necessity and beauty of his plan of salvation, and in his call to join in his transformative purposes for every corner of his world.

Today the team at LICC works with Christians and leaders from across the denominations. Their aim is to help Christians make a difference for Christ out on their daily frontlines, to help church leaders help them, and to help theological educators train church leaders for this central calling of Christ to make fruitful whole-life disciples for the whole of life – for the blessing of our nation and the salvation of many.

LICC's website is packed full of articles, videos, stories, and resources to equip you for daily life as a disciple of Christ.

Visit **licc.org.uk**

mail@licc.org.uk
+44 20 7399 9555

St Peter's
Vere Street
London, W1G 0DQ

[fusion]

About Fusion

Fusion are committed to championing student mission.
They believe in the power and potency of students as a force for
revival and transformation in the world and recognise that university
is a key formational, decision-making time for them. They are
convinced that it is the local church who are best placed to nurture,
disciple and support students into mission across campuses, cities
and beyond. Fusion therefore seek to equip students for a life
of mission and discipleship by guiding them into local churches
who are then trained and resourced to effectively care for and
release students into the calling God has placed on their lives.

Fusion's website is packed full of resources, blog post, stories, videos,
and ideas to help students live a life of mission at university.

Visit **fusionmovement.org**

hello@fusionmovement.org
+44 15 0926 8505

Unit 7, 30 Meadow Lane
Loughborough
Leicestershire, LE11 1JY

IT'S A JUNGLE OUT THERE. AN AWESOME, BEAUTIFUL JUNGLE.

Most students leave university in a flurry of exam sweat, half-packed boxes, and last hurrahs.

That is, without a lot of spiritual preparation.

Instead, we plunge into the working world believing a lot of myths: that God is mostly for church and quiet-time, that business means business, that we have only one calling, and that we should have it all together.

Routed helps break down these myths.

This small group study is the ultimate prep for life post-uni. Over the four sessions, a group will tackle:

- **God's interest in the whole of life**
- **Being faithful in our work**
- **Choosing work wisely**
- **Navigating change well**

Routed: Journeying into Work with God gives students a vision for life after uni, laying out biblical mindsets and practical steps for whole-life discipleship through Bible study, discussion, video segments featuring real-life stories, and exercises for self-reflection and prayer.

In addition to this workbook, *Routed: Journeying into Work with God* includes a leader's guide and eight content videos, available free at licc.org.uk/routed.

Also available

LAUNCHED

Launched is Routed's sister resource – a group study for freshers on whole-life discipleship at uni.

A resource from

licc. | [fusion]

ISBN 978-0-9928190-6-4

9 780992 819064